30 Days to Unlocking Inner Joy & Peace after a Breakup

Sheryl Nicole Prince

DEDICATION

This book is dedicated to all of the beautiful souls with huge hearts that courageously give love so freely. You are loving, lovable, and loved.

Table of Contents

ACKNOWLEDGMENTS

Thank you Father God for your unconditional love, grace and mercy. You've been my rock and have kept me together when I felt like I was falling apart. Through your son Jesus Christ, you've given me access to joy, peace, and love like no other. I am forever grateful for your many blessings.

A special thanks to my loved ones who have supported me along this journey. Your love and support mean more than words can express. I love you all beyond measure.

1 Declare

We've all been there before, cruising down "Lovers Lane" only to end in a fiery crash & burn on "Heartbreak Highway". How did we get here? More importantly, how do we pick up the pieces and move on?

Moving on begins with a decision. Intentionally deciding to move on from heartache to healing so that you can experience true joy, peace & love.

So let's begin! Write the following statement and post it on your mirror. Every time you lay eyes on it, repeat it out aloud.

"Today I declare my decision to move on from heartache to healing because I'm worth it. I deserve joy, peace, and love."

Reflect on the declaration you made. What are your thoughts and feelings about moving on? What are your hopes and fears?

_____

_____

_____

_____

_____
_____
_____
_____
_____
_____
_____
_____
_____
_____
_____
_____
_____
_____
_____
_____
_____
_____

2 Purge: Actions Speak Louder Than Words

It's one thing to say you're moving on, but it's a whole other thing to actually do it. Why, because letting go is hard. But it's necessary in order to move forward.

We're not just gonna talk about it, we're gonna be about it. Let's put some action behind the declaration we made yesterday. Start by deleting your ex's phone number, texts, emails, pictures, etc. Unfollow him/her on social media. Get rid of any and everything that reminds you of him/her. Yes, it's time to purge! I know it's hard, but take a deep breath in and inhale power. Now exhale the pain and get to purging!

After your purge, take a moment of silence and then jot down your deepest, rawest thoughts and feelings.

_____
_____
_____
_____
_____
_____
_____

3 Release: Let It Out

You probably woke up this morning thinking "What have I done?!" Why did I get rid of all the traces of my past with you know who? (Insert crying emoji) Been there, felt that. I was on a "high" while deleting and blocking. But when reality set in, I felt super low. The finality of our breakup hit me like a ton of bricks. All I wanted to do was crawl under a rock and disappear.

But that's not how life works so I had to fight the feeling, literally. Kickboxing is one hell of a drug for me. It's a great workout and allows me to release pent up anger and frustration. I absolutely love kickboxing!

What helps you let it all out? Writing? Dancing? Exercising? Whatever it is (as long as it's legal & not detrimental to your health), I want you to engage in that activity today and then journal about your experience afterwards.

Describe exactly what you did and how it made you feel afterwards. Were you able to let it all out and *WOOSAH*?

4 Truth: Facts Over Feelings

Yesterday was all about letting it out. Sometimes you need a good "woosah" moment so that you can blow off some steam. But let's be real, breakups are hard and take time to fully get over. For days, weeks, months and even years sometimes, it's all you can think about. Some days are better than others. Other days are downright miserable and may seem unbearable.

That's when you have to fight your feelings. Face the facts and get out of your feelings. He/she wasn't right for you. He/she didn't value you. He/she cheated on you. Whatever the case was, the fact of the matter is it's over for a reason.

Now let's get out of our feelings and confront the facts head on. Make a t-chart as shown below:

Write what you're feeling and then write a corresponding fact. For example, "I'm missing him like crazy" (feeling). "He didn't even have the courtesy to respond to the text message I sent him 6 days ago" (fact). Now review your list and reflect on how looking at the facts affect your feelings.

_____

_____

_____

10

_____
_____
_____
_____
_____
_____
_____
_____
_____
_____
_____
_____
_____
_____
_____
_____
_____

.

5 Recharge

You're probably feeling all sorts of out of it—mentally, emotionally & physically. It's quite common to feel depleted when you're going through a rough time.

You know what you need? A good "pick me up" to the rescue! You need something that will recharge your battery. Make a list of things that will give you that spark back. Then, choose one thing from the list and JUST DO IT (in my Nike voice). Will it be a spa day, a mani-pedi, retail therapy or something else?

Whatever you decide, enjoy it to the fullest then write about the affect the activity had on your mood.

_____

_____

_____

_____

_____

_____

_____

_____

_____

_____
_____
_____
_____
_____
_____
_____
_____
_____
_____
_____
_____
_____

6 Rediscover Your Identity

Often times when we're involved in a relationship we inadvertently lose a part of ourselves. We get so caught up with our partner that our identities become intertwined so to speak.

Remember, whether you're involved or single, YOU. ARE. UNIQUELY. YOU. That being said, it's time to reclaim your identity! List the qualities, traits, and/or characteristics that make you uniquely you.

After reviewing your list, write an introduction reintroducing yourself to the world. Be authentic, be descriptive, be creative, and BE YOU.

_____
_____
_____
_____
_____
_____
_____
_____
_____

7 Reclaim Your Time

It's not uncommon to become so involved with your significant other that most of your free time is invested spent with him/her. Especially if you're like me and your love language is "quality time". I'd spend every free moment with my significant other if I could.

Not only is that not possible, it's not healthy. You each need time and room to breathe and live your lives independent from one another. There's no better time than being newly single to reclaim your time.

What do you enjoy doing in your free time? What are your hobbies and interests? Make a list of them and choose 1 or 2 things to engage in today. Then reflect on your time spent doing what you enjoy. Describe how it felt to reclaim your time.

_____

_____

_____

_____

_____

_____
_____
_____
_____
_____
_____
_____
_____
_____
_____
_____
_____
_____
_____
_____
_____
_____
_____
_____
—

8 Realign with Your Passion

I don't know about you, but at times I'm guilty of getting so wrapped up in my relationship that I neglect the things I'm passionate about. Don't get me wrong, my world doesn't revolve around my significant other but as I've mentioned previously, quality time is my love language so a huge chunk of my free time was spent with my significant other. Sometimes I'd put off things in order to spend time with him, then I'd be forced to play catch up on work, projects, etc. My passion was suffering so to speak because of what/who I gave priority to.

It's all about balance. There has to be a healthy balance between how much time you invest in your partner and how much time you invest in yourself. You matter. Your passion(s) matters. What are you passionate about? What have you been sacrificing by putting on the back burner for the sake of love?

Today declare that your passion(s) will no longer take a backseat to anyone or anything. Make a post of this declaration on your social media wall. Then reflect on how making this public declaration made you feel and note the feedback you received. Detail how you plan to move forward with pursuing your passion from here on out.

9 Reconnect with Family & Friends

You know that friend that is "acting brand new" because they got a new boo? You just might be that friend. I know, you're not acting brand new, you're just enjoying the companionship of your partner and y'all love. But sometimes friends and family don't see it that way. You're not as available, always with you know who, or just don't have time for them anymore. You don't mean to be this way but you're in love and it's y'all against the world.

It doesn't have to be that way. Once again, this is where balance is needed. Yes, spend as much time as you can being in love and what not. But also make time for those that love you. Because at the end of the day, they'll always be there (hopefully) even if ole boy or ole girl exits stage left.

Call a loved one that you haven't spoken to in while. Simply check-in and reconnect. Perhaps make plans to meet up soon. If you feel comfortable enough, get their feedback about how they viewed your last relationship. Do they feel it changed you? Write about your experience reconnecting with your loved one and your thoughts on the feedback they provided (if any).

_____
_____
_____
_____
_____
_____
_____
_____
_____
_____
_____
_____
_____
_____
_____
_____
_____
_____
_____
_____
_____

10 Reflect

We're a third of the way along our journey. We've made powerful declarations, purged, faced the facts, realigned with who we are & what we're passionate about, and reconnected with our loved ones. I'm sure it's been a roller coaster of emotions over these past few days. The ups and downs are sure to have weighed heavily upon you.

Today let's take the opportunity to reflect on our journey so far. Take a moment to sit in stillness and simply reflect on what this experience has been like for you thus far. Have you noticed any changes? What thoughts are going through your head? What expectations do you have? Allow yourself to think deeply and freely. Jot down a few profound thoughts that surfaced.

_____
_____
_____
_____
_____
_____
_____

11 Time is of the Essence

They say time heals all wounds. But it seems like it takes forever to get that once special person out of your system. Minutes, hours, days, weeks, and months don't go by fast enough. You just want to be over that person like yesterday. But the feelings seem to linger forever.

How do you get him/her out of your system? Especially when time doesn't seem to be on your side. Perhaps spending time doing what you enjoy or exploring something new will preoccupy your mind and your time.

So beginning today, carve out time for something you enjoy. Exercising, reading a good book, engaging in a hobby, or whatever your "thing" is. Or be adventurous and try something new. Learn a new skill, meet new people, or simply try your hand at something out of the ordinary. Write about your experience and note whether or not it helped you get out of that frame of mind.

\

Sometimes when relationships don't work out for whatever reason, we internalize it and get down on ourselves. WE must be the reason or the cause. So we beat upon ourselves mercilessly.

That's both damaging and harmful. It effects your perception of self and lowers your self-esteem. It can even lead to depression and you devaluing yourself. That's unhealthy and the worst thing possible given your fragile state.

Let's combat those thoughts as soon they surface. In fact, talk back to them and over them. Speak light into darkness, speak positivity in opposition to negativity. When that voice utters *You're the reason it didn't work*, tell it *We didn't work because WE didn't make it work*. When that voice says *You're not good enough,* counter with *I'm more than enough*.

Don't let the voice overpower you. Don't internalize and claim what doesn't belong to you. Talk back and take control! Write every negative thought that pops in your mind in pencil. Counter it with something positive. Simply write it in pen over your initial negative thought. Then reflect on how this exercise challenged and/or changed you.

_____
_____
_____
_____
_____
_____
_____
_____
_____
_____
_____
_____

13 I Love You

Self-love is a beautiful thing. It allows us to know and experience what true love is and accept nothing less than that.

I know it's been hella rough these last few days. You're probably feeling down about yourself and beating yourself up. We're not going to have that for one second.

I want you to love on yourself like you've never loved on yourself before. Don't be afraid to compliment yourself and admire all there is to admire about yourself. Go ahead, stand in the mirror and just lavish on the love. Afterwards, jot down 3 things that resonated most during this exercise and explain why.

_____

_____

_____

_____

_____

_____

_____

_____

14 Dear Self

I hope you woke up this morning with a smile on your face and your spirits lifted. Sometimes all we need is a little love. Other times we need a lot of love.

That's why we're gonna pretty much pick up where we left off and turn up the dial. Today, we affirm who the hell we are. Yup, I said what I said (in my Nene voice).

"Dear Self, in case you didn't know or you somehow forgot, you are hella dope." That's how I'm starting my affirmations today. How will you start? Dig deep within yourself and just pull it out. List at least 5 things you need to tell/remind yourself in the form of a positive affirmation. Ready, set, AFFIRM!!!

_____

_____
_____
_____
_____
_____
_____
_____
_____

_____
_____
_____
_____
_____
_____
_____
_____
_____
_____
_____
_____
_____
_____
_____
_____
_____
_____
_____
_____
_____
_____
_____
_____
_____
_____

.

15 Bigger Picture

There's a saying that goes a little something like this, "There's a lid for every pot". Maybe you weren't the lid for that particular pot. But that doesn't diminish your value nonetheless. You're still a prized lid for a deserving pot.

Unfortunately or perhaps fortunately, things didn't work out between you and your ex. That doesn't change who you are and the value you hold. It just means you two weren't a good fit for whatever reason.

Today I want to challenge you to think long, hard and truthfully about why you and your ex weren't a good fit. Write down your thoughts. Remember, it's not about diminishing who either of you are as people. It's merely an exercise to help you see the bigger picture.

_____
_____
_____
_____
_____
_____

16 Dear Ex

Have you ever missed someone so much it hurt so bad? I've experienced it and it's one of the worst feelings. You miss seeing that person, talking to him/her, spending time with him/her, etc. It's especially hard when you've established a routine with someone then things suddenly change.

Seemingly overnight you have to get used to not having that person in your life. It almost takes every fiber of your being not to crawl back to the comfort zone you've established with him/her. You're forced to let go and move on. But there may be some unresolved things. Things you need to get off your chest.

So that's exactly what we're going to do today. We're releasing the things bombarding our minds and weighing heavily on our hearts. Write a letter to your ex expressing every single thing you need to get out of your system. Don't hold anything back, let it all out. Afterwards, tear the letter into the smallest pieces possible and sprinkle them into the trash where they belong. Be sure to record your thoughts and feelings after this exercise.

17 Free Yourself

Forgiving someone who hurt you is not easy at all. But it's necessary in order to heal, grow and move on. Forgiveness is about freeing yourself. It's for you, not the other person.

Begin by forgiving yourself. You may have put up with things you didn't deserve. Forgive yourself. You may not have been the best version of yourself. Forgive yourself. No matter what it is, forgive yourself.

Now extend this same forgiveness to your ex. Forgive him/her for hurting you. Forgive him/her for not loving you properly. Pen a letter to your ex detailing your vow to forgive him/her. Don't share the letter with your ex. It's for your safe keeping to remind you of your decision to free yourself by forgiving them.

_____
_____
_____
_____
_____
_____
_____

_____

_____

_____

_____

_____

_____

_____

_____

_____

_____

_____

_____

_____

_____

_____

_____

_____

_____

_____

_____

_____

_____

_____

_____

18 Take Control

Have you given others control over your happiness? Was your ex the main source of your happiness or lack thereof? If you answered yes to either question, it's time to take back the remote control to your life.

Life is what you make it. Sounds cliché but it's so true. If you want happiness, create it. It's as simple as that.

For today's exercise, I want you to define happiness and identity how you can create it. Don't just write it, live it. Application is key.

_____

_____

_____

_____

_____

_____

_____

_____

_____

19 Who Am I?

Just as we can choose happiness, we can choose how the world views us. Why not choose to be the best version of ourselves. Begin by defining who we are. Not who you're told to be by others/the world, but who YOU say you are.

Who are you? What makes you uniquely you? What words describe who you are as an individual? Brainstorm a list of words/phrases that describe you. Not your profession, not your role(s) but YOU. Now write a declarative statement about who you are and post it as your bio on your social media pages.

_____

_____

_____

_____

_____

_____

_____

_____

_____

_____

_____

_____
_____
_____
_____
_____
_____
_____
_____
_____
_____
_____
_____
_____
_____
_____
_____
_____
_____
_____
_____
_____
_____
_____
_____
_____
_____
_____
_____
_____
_____

_____

_____

_____

_____

_____

_____

_____

_____

_____

20 Check-In Time

Woot, woot, we're 2/3 through our journey. You're probably both exhausted and excited at the same time. This last leg is extremely important so let's prepare accordingly.

Take the opportunity today to reflect on your journey so far. Take a moment to sit in stillness and simply think about what this experience has been like for you thus far. How has it changed you? What are you struggling with? What do you anticipate moving forward? Allow yourself to think deeply and freely. Afterwards, jot down a few profound thoughts that surfaced.

_____

_____

_____

_____

_____

_____

_____

_____

_____

_____

When I'm feeling down and in the dumps, helping others truly lifts my spirits. Extending myself to someone in need brings such joy and is so fulfilling. Not only is it rewarding, it helps me put my energy to good use.

Today, I want you to selflessly love on others. See a need, fulfill it. Or perhaps treat someone to something nice (think lunch or coffee, don't splurge). Even better, volunteer for a community service project. Whatever you do, do it out of love because you are loving, thus lovable and loved.

Write about how your act of love altered your perspective on your current situation.

_____

_____

_____

_____

_____

_____

_____

_____

_____

_____

_____

_____

_____

_____

_____

_____

_____

_____

Unfortunately, sometimes when others (especially those that we care most about) don't see our true value, we begin to devalue ourselves. I'm here to tell you that you matter. Your value doesn't decrease because someone else doesn't recognize it. You're enough and deserving of someone who appreciates your value.

This very moment declare that you matter. List the reasons why you matter and the great value you possess. Make a recording of your declaration and adopt it as your anthem. Reflect on your experience completing this exercise and explain how you'll incorporate it into your daily routine.

_____
_____
_____
_____
_____
_____
_____
_____
_____

_____

_____

_____

_____

_____

_____

_____

_____

_____

_____

_____

23 Encourage Others

We should always be kind to others because we never know what they're going through. People you see every day are fighting battles you know nothing of and vice versa. Sometimes we need to be the light that we seek.

Take out time today to speak with someone about how they're doing. Avoid surface level conversation. Go deeper and really take the time to listen and understand them. Offer up words of encouragement. Share inspirational quotes, scriptures, etc. Speak light into darkness.

Did you feel encouraged as you were encouraging others? Write your thoughts and feelings following this exercise.

_____
_____
_____
_____
_____
_____
_____

_____
_____
_____
_____
_____
_____
_____
_____
_____
_____
_____
_____
_____
_____

24 Intentional Joy

Who says you can't be intentional when it comes to being joyful? No one, exactly! In fact, you should be VERY intentional in this area of your life. True joy is like nothing you've ever experienced. It fills you up and gives so much meaning to your life.

Don't you want to experience that? Don't you want to live a life of joy and share it with the world? Who wouldn't?! So from this moment forth be intentional about producing joy in your life. Your thoughts, words, and actions should be aligned with joy. Remember, joy comes from within and shouldn't easily be affected by external factors.

How will you be intentional about living a life filled with joy?

_____
_____
_____
_____
_____
_____
_____

_____
_____
_____
_____
_____
_____
_____
_____
_____
_____
_____
_____
_____
_____

25 Choose Joy

Sometimes life throws some hard-hurled curveballs your way. They can steal your joy if you let them. But you're intentional about having joy in your life so they don't stand a chance.

How can you have joy in the face of adversity? It's definitely not easy but it's doable. Choose joy, ferociously defeating attempted joy stealers.

List the usual suspects (things & people) who attempt to steal your joy. Write an "action plan" to counter their attack. For example, during my commute I need my gospel music to help me deal with the crazy folks on the roads. Get the gist, now get to it!

_____
_____
_____
_____
_____
_____
_____
_____

26 Peace Please

If I had to choose between winning the lotto and having peace, I'd choose peace in a heartbeat. Yup, you heard that right. There's no amount of money that can equate to peace. Peace is priceless.

How do you achieve peace? Just as you're intentional about being joyful, you must be intentional about peace. What does peace look like to you? How does it make you feel? Use your words to paint a clear picture of what perfect peace is.

_____
_____
_____
_____
_____
_____
_____
_____
_____
_____
_____
_____
_____

27 Unshakable Peace

Just as there are joy stealers, there are peace killers. But you already know that you're more than equipped to fight back.

In this life, things are going to happen. What's most important is how you react and respond, as opposed to what actually happens. In it all and through it all, don't allow your peace to waver. Regardless of what happens, choose peace; peace of mind, peace in your heart, and being peaceful towards others.

How can you experience peace that's so deeply rooted external forces/factors have no control over it? Just as you devised an "action plan" to combat joy stealers, create one for peace killers. Simply identify and eliminate the usual suspects that threaten your peace.

_____

_____

_____

_____

_____

_____

_____

_____

The feelings may still be raw and the pain may still sting, but every day it gets a little better. It's totally okay to acknowledge how you feel. You're not expected to "get over it" overnight. It takes time and has to run its course.

However, operating from a place of intentional joy and peace ensures that we're grounded and focused. It also allows us to heal and move on.

Take out time to face some hard truths today. Assert how you won't let them define you or undo the progress you've made. For example, "I've been feeling lonely lately but I have peace knowing that I'm not alone. I have family and friends who love me dearly and are here for me. Most importantly, I love myself enough to not settle for less than what I deserve because I am valuable and worthy."

Now it's your turn...

_____
_____
_____
_____

_____
_____
_____
_____
_____
_____
_____
_____
_____
_____
_____
_____
_____
_____
_____
_____
_____

29 Mirror, Mirror

Mirrors show us our reflection. What you see is standing right in front of you. Very superficial. What you don't see is what's hidden beneath the surface.
Much like an iceberg. You see the tip which doesn't compare to the huge mass that's covered by the depths of the water.

Over the course of these past few weeks you've done a lot of digging and excavating to uncover what lies deep within. You open-mindedly engaged in exercises that stretched and challenged you, but facilitated the healing process. You've pushed pass hurt, pain, discomfort, etc. to unlock the keys to your inner joy and peace.

What have you learned about yourself during the course of this journey? What have you uncovered? What have you overcome? What unresolved issues remain? What are your next steps? Think carefully about the answers to these questions, then pen a thoughtful letter to yourself detailing your self-discovery. Post your letter on your mirror as a daily reminder of how far you've come.

SHERYL NICOLE PRINCE

_____

_____

_____

_____

_____

_____

_____

_____

_____

_____

_____

_____

_____

_____

_____

_____

_____

30 Celebration Time

Woot, woot, you did it!!! Congratulations for staying the course on this sometimes difficult journey. You've experienced a roller coaster ride of emotions—ups, downs, twists, turns, etc. But you saw it through to the end nonetheless. Hopefully you've learned some valuable things about yourself along the way.

Let's take a moment to celebrate your amazing accomplishment. Do something nice for yourself, share your experience with someone or simply reflect on your progress over a well-deserved glass of wine. Whatever you do, relish in the moment because you truly deserve it.

But first, let's capture some goodies for the record book. What was your highest point? What was your lowest point? Which exercise was the most challenging? Which exercise produced the most profound impact? How has this journey affected/changed you?

Whew, now go celebrate the new and improved YOU!!!

ABOUT THE AUTHOR

Sheryl Nicole Prince is an educator, entrepreneur, and author. Over the past 15 years she's worked assiduously in the field of special education assuming various roles and leadership positions. For the past 2 years, Sheryl has energetically explored her entrepreneurial spirit. In January 2017, she launched *Diverse Destinations*, a home-based travel agency that specializes in planning group excursions. In the spring of 2017, she launched *Sheryl Nicole*, a lifestyle brand that inspires and empowers others to live a life of purpose, on purpose. Sheryl is currently working on launching her 3rd business venture, a comprehensive educational services agency that caters to the unique needs of each individual family.

Outside of her many endeavors, Sheryl enjoys alone time with God, spending quality time with loved ones, and traveling.

71695578R00059

Made in the USA
Columbia, SC
27 August 2019